CliffsNotes™

Ethan Frome

By Suzanne Pavlos, M.Ed.

IN THIS BOOK

- Probe the Life and Background of the Author
- Preview the novel in the Introduction to the Novel
- Discover the themes in the Critical Commentaries
- Examine in-depth Character Analyses
- Explore the significance of the work with Critical Essays
- Reinforce what you learn with CliffsNotes Review
- Find additional information to further your study in CliffsNotes Resource Center and online at www.cliffsnotes.com

WILEY

Wiley Publishing, Inc.

About the Author
Suzanne Pavlos taught high school English and reading. She is currently a freelance writer and editor and working as a psychotherapist.

Publisher's Acknowledgments
Editorial
Project Editor: Kathleen A. Dobie
Acquisitions Editor: Gregory W. Tubach
Copy Editor: Robert Annis

Glossary Editors: The editors and staff at Webster's New World™ Dictionaries
Editorial Administrator: Michelle Hacker
Editorial Assistant: Jennifer Young

Production
Indexer: York Production Services, Inc.
Proofreader: York Production Services, Inc.
Wiley Indianapolis Composition Services

Published by:
Wiley Publishing, Inc.
909 Third Avenue
New York, NY 10022
www.wiley.com

Table of Contents

How to Use This Book

CliffsNotes *Ethan Frome* supplements the original work, giving you background information about the author, an introduction to the novel, a graphical character map, critical commentaries, expanded glossaries, and a comprehensive index. CliffsNotes Review tests your comprehension of the original text and reinforces learning with questions and answers, practice projects, and more. For further information on Edith Wharton and *Ethan Frome*, check out the CliffsNotes Resource Center.

CliffsNotes provides the following icons to highlight essential elements of particular interest:

Reveals the underlying themes in the work.

Helps you to more easily relate to or discover the depth of a character.

Uncovers elements such as setting, atmosphere, mystery, passion, violence, irony, symbolism, tragedy, foreshadowing, and satire.

Enables you to appreciate the nuances of words and phrases.

Don't Miss Our Web Site

Discover classic literature as well as modern-day treasures by visiting the CliffsNotes Web site at www.cliffsnotes.com. You can obtain a quick download of a CliffsNotes title, purchase a title in print form, browse our catalog, or view online samples.

You'll also find interactive tools that are fun and informative, links to interesting Web sites, tips, articles, and additional resources to help you, not only for literature, but for test prep, finance, careers, computers, and Internet too. See you at www.cliffsnotes.com!

LIFE AND BACKGROUND OF THE AUTHOR

Personal Background

Edith Wharton, an American author and Pulitzer Prize winner, is known for her ironic and polished prose about the aristocratic New York society into which she was born. Her protagonists are most often tragic heroes or heroines portrayed as intelligent and emotional people who want more out of life. Wharton's protagonists challenge social taboos, but are unable to overcome the barriers of social convention. Wharton's personal experiences, opinions, and passions influenced her writing.

Edith Wharton was born Edith Newbold Jones on January 24, 1862, in New York City to George Frederic Jones and Lucretia Stevens Rhinelander Jones. Her family on both sides was established, old-money New York business aristocracy. Her ancestry was of the best English and Dutch strains. Edith had two older brothers: Frederic Rhinelander Jones (Freddie), sixteen years older than her, and Henry Edward Jones (Harry), eleven years older. Because her brothers went to boarding school, and so were often away from home, Edith was essentially raised as an only child in a brownstone mansion on West Twenty-third Street in New York City. The Jones family frequently took trips to the country and to Europe. From the beginning of her life, Edith was immersed in a society noted for its manners, taste, snobbishness, and long list of social do's and don'ts.

Education and Early Work

Edith did not attend school; according to the custom of the day for well-to-do young women, she was taught at home by her governess and tutors. She became proficient in French, German, and Italian. The books in her father's large library became her passion. She read English and French literature by Jonathan Swift, Daniel Defoe, William Shakespeare, John Milton, Jean Racine, Jean La Fontaine, and Victor Hugo. She read all of Johann Goethe's plays and poems and the poetry of John Keats and Percy Bysshe Shelley. Edith was fascinated with stories and began composing them herself when she was a child; she called the process "making-up." Her parents did not encourage her writing; however, after Henry Wadsworth Longfellow recommended that several of Edith's poems be published in the *Atlantic Monthly* magazine, her parents recognized her talent and had a volume of her poems (entitled *Verses*) privately published. A year later, when Edith was only sixteen years old, she completed a 30,000 word novella entitled *Fast and Loose*, a story about manners that mocks high society.

At the age of seventeen, Edith was immersed in her books. She spent her time studying, reading, and writing and was indifferent to people her own age. Worried about Edith, her parents decided that she should make her debut in society. Despite her natural shyness, she was a social success. In August 1882, at the age of nineteen, Edith became engaged to Harry Stevens, a prominent figure in New York society. By October of the same year, the engagement was broken as a result of meddling by the mothers of the engaged couple.

Married Life

On April 29, 1885, Edith married Edward R. "Teddy" Wharton, a friend of her brother. Teddy, who was thirteen years older than Edith, was from a socially acceptable Boston family. After their wedding, the Whartons settled in New York City and soon purchased a home in Newport, Rhode Island. Teddy supported them both on his inherited income, which made it possible for the couple to live in New York and Newport, and to travel to Europe frequently. In 1902, they moved into their mansion, "The Mount," in Lenox, Massachusetts. Having collaborated with architect Ogden Codman on a book entitled *The Decoration of Houses* (1897), Edith put her knowledge to use and provided input regarding the design of the mansion as well as the interior decoration.

Though they were intellectually and sexually incompatible, the Whartons lived a companionable and expensive life, traveling back and forth between Europe and the United States. During the first years of Edith's marriage to Teddy, he was a companion to her and secured her position in the aristocratic society that she denounced, yet valued, throughout her life. Soon, however, events began to cloud their marriage. As Edith's writing abilities increased, so did her reputation. During the 1890's Edith wrote short stories for *Scribner's Magazine*, published *The Valley of Decision* (1902), a historical novel, and *The House of Mirth* (1905). She spent a considerable amount of time with would-be and genuine literary personalities and Teddy found himself in the background of Edith's life. His health and mental stability became progressively worse and required increasingly prolonged therapeutic trips to Europe. In 1907, the Whartons settled in France in the fashionable Rue de Varenne. While Edith's marital relationship (which had never been an intimate one) began to fall apart, she continued to write. Her tragic love story, *Ethan Frome*, was published in 1911 to much success and acclaim. Eventually, Edith and Teddy began living apart, and in 1913, Edith divorced Teddy because of his unstable mental health and acts of adultery. Edith was also guilty of adultery. She had an affair with Morton Fullerton, a journalist for the *London Times* and friend of Henry James. (James, an American novelist, was a lifelong friend of Edith's. His writing style, known as *American realism*, influenced Edith's own writing.)

The French Years

After her divorce, Edith continued to visit the United States to retain her American citizenship, even though she chose to live permanently in France. During World War I, Edith established two organizations for war refugees: the Children of Flanders and the American Hostel for Refugees. She also made several visits to the French front where she distributed medical supplies and made observations from which she wrote war essays influencing Americans to support the Allied cause. Edith's war essays appeared in the book, *Fighting France, from Dunkerque to Belfort* (1915). As a fund-raiser she organized *The Book of the Homeless* (1916), an illustrated anthology of war writings by well-known authors and artists of the time. Edith won the French Legion of Honor and was awarded many decorations by the French and Belgian governments for her contributions to charity. She continued her charitable efforts after the war by providing aid to tubercular patients in France.

In 1919, Edith purchased two homes in France: the chateau Ste. Claire in Hyeres, and the Pavillon Colombe, located north of Paris. Both homes had elaborate gardens where Edith immersed herself. Because she felt as though she had been cut off from the life she knew before the war, she was anxious to re-establish friendships and stability. She began entertaining well-known literary personalities such as Walter Berry, Robert Norton, Percy Lubbock, Paul Bourget, and of course, her close friend Henry James.

Edith continued to write until her death in Hyeres, France on August 11, 1937 at the age of 75. She was buried in a cemetery at Versailles in France. All of Edith's papers and unfinished work were given to Yale University with the stipulation that certain of them not be released until 1968.

Career Highlights

After publishing her first volume of short stories, *The Greater Inclination* in 1899, Edith produced numerous novels, travel books, short stories (including many ghost stories), and poems. Several of Edith's novels have been made into successful plays and motion pictures by other writers.

Edith is perhaps best known for her novels depicting New York aristocratic life and the complicated struggle of the individual with the conventions of a powerful, and triumphant, moneyed class.

Edith received much acclaim for her lifelong devotion to writing. She is considered one of the leading American authors of the twentieth century. Because of her humanitarian endeavors and contributions to literature, Edith became the first woman to receive an honorary doctorate from Yale University in 1923, and in 1930 she was elected to the American Academy of Arts and Letters.

INTRODUCTION TO THE NOVEL

Introduction

Wharton began the story that became *Ethan Frome* in the early 1900s as an exercise in writing for a tutor she hired to improve her French conversational skills. She based the tale on her experiences of several summers' residence at the Wharton country home in Lenox, Massachusetts. The early form of the story is three chapters of straight narration in French without prologue or epilogue; Mattie and "Hart" (Ethan) know they love each other at the beginning of the story, and after "Anna's" (Zeena's) visit to town to hire a girl as Mattie's replacement, the lovers are forced to part. Waiting for the train to take her away, Hart swears to desert Anna and follow Mattie; Mattie emphatically rejects this idea, and so the French version ends.

Wharton put aside the French tale for a few years and when she approached it again, she made radical changes in structure and theme. Most obviously, she added the device of a *frame narrative*—bracketing the main story with an epilogue and prologue written in first person. The idea of a frame narrative was clearly taken from Robert Browning's *The Ring and the Book* and from a short story of Honoré de Balzac's, "La Grande Bretêche." Balzac's story is about a traveler who visits a small village and becomes fascinated with an old house. Wishing to find out about it (as The Narrator of *Ethan Frome* is made curious when he sees Ethan leaving the post office), Balzac's traveler asks the villagers about the house, and the story is gradually put together by compiling a composite of different bits of information. In theme, *Ethan Frome's* vision of frustration, catastrophe, and prolonged pain and despair reflects a maturity and complexity of thought not apparent in the earlier vignette Wharton composed in French.

Serialized in *Scribner's Magazine* from August to October in 1911, *Ethan Frome* was published in book form the same year. Popular response was enthusiastic, and critics and reviewers praised the finely crafted structure as well as the bleak, naturalistic vision of New England country life. The book showed that Wharton's talents were by no means limited to novels of New York society manners. Wharton used the New England locale again in a novel, *Summer* (1917), and a short story, "The Bunner Sisters." As in *Ethan Frome*, the two later efforts show the stifling effect of the environment on individuals who try without success to break away and then fall back into smothering frustration and despair.

A Brief Synopsis

Wharton wrote *Ethan Frome* as a *frame story*—meaning that the prologue and epilogue constitute a "frame" around the main story. The "frame" is The Narrator's vision of the tragedy that befalls Ethan Frome. The frame story takes place nearly twenty years after the events of the main story and is written in first person, revealing the thoughts and feelings of The Narrator. The main story, which describes the three and a half days before and including Ethan and Mattie's sledding accident, is written in third person—an omniscient narration that allows Wharton to relate the thoughts and feelings of all the characters.

Ethan Frome begins when The Narrator, an engineer who is living temporarily in Starkfield, Massachusetts while working on a project in a nearby town, becomes curious about Ethan Frome. The Narrator questions his landlady, Mrs. Ned Hale, and Harmon Gow, a long-time resident and former stagecoach driver, about Ethan. They provide The Narrator with bits and pieces of information about Ethan, which make him even more intrigued with the story of Ethan's life.

Temporarily unable to get to and from the train station in Corbury Flats, The Narrator acts on Gow's suggestion and asks Ethan to transport him back and forth. After a week of riding with Ethan, The Narrator and Ethan are caught in a blinding snowstorm on their return to Starkfield. Ethan invites The Narrator to spend the night at his farmhouse. During his unexpected stay with Ethan, The Narrator is able to glean information about Ethan's life.

As a young man, Ethan Frome wanted to become an engineer. He left home, attended a technological college in Worcester, Massachusetts, and spent time in Florida actually working on a small engineering job. His dream was to settle in a metropolitan area where he could take advantage of the opportunities city life offered. Unfortunately, Ethan's studies (as well as his dreams) come to an abrupt halt when his father died and his mother became ill soon afterwards. He returned to Starkfield, Massachusetts to care for his mother and to run the family farm and sawmill. Realizing that he couldn't do everything by himself, he made arrangements for his cousin Zenobia (Zeena) Pierce to live with them. Zeena took over the care of Ethan's mother as well as the household duties. After his mother's death, Ethan couldn't imagine being alone again on the farm, so he married Zeena.

In an attempt to reclaim his dreams and move to a metropolitan area, Ethan tried to sell the farm, but his efforts were unsuccessful. After a year of marriage, Zeena became well known to the people in Stark-field for her "sickliness." She suffered from a myriad of illnesses and her disposition became irritable and disagreeable. Ethan's dreams were doomed.

As the main story begins, Mattie Silver, a cousin of Zeena's whose parents' deaths left her destitute, has been a part of the Frome household for a year. Although Mattie is grateful to have a roof over her head and work as an aide to her cousin, she is, however, quite forgetful and often spends time dreaming rather than working. As a result, Ethan, who has secretly fallen in love with Mattie, completes many of her chores.

Three days before the "smash-up," Ethan goes one evening to meet Mattie, who is socializing at a church dance, and walk her home. He feels jealous when he observes Denis Eady, a local grocer and propri-etor of the livery stable, flirting and dancing with Mattie. After Mattie refuses a ride home with Eady, she and Ethan walk home arm-in-arm.

The next day, Zeena tells Ethan that she's going to Bettsbridge to see Doctor Buck and spending the night with her Aunt Martha Pierce. Zeena asks Ethan to drive her to the train station, but Ethan tells her that he can't because he's going to see Andrew Hale, owner of a con-struction company in Starkfield, to get paid for lumber he sold him. He suggests that Jotham Powell, a man who helps out around the Frome farm, drive her to the train station. Because Ethan had no intention of seeing Hale, he absolves his guilt about lying to Zeena by actually going to see Hale and asking for an advance on his load of lumber. As Ethan expects, Hale declines to pay him then.

That evening, Mattie makes a particularly nice supper for Ethan. She even uses one of Zeena's best dishes, made of red glass, which is stored on the top shelf in the china closet. During the dinner, the cat knocks Zeena's red dish off the table and it breaks on the floor. Ethan pieces the dish together, puts it back on the shelf in the china closet, and promises to glue it together before Zeena returns home. The rest of the evening Ethan and Mattie spend the evening conversing with each other, well content in each other's company.

The following day, Ethan rushes through his work, then home to glue the red dish together before Zeena returns home. To his surprise, when he gets home with the glue, Zeena is already there. Zeena informs Ethan that she has "complications" and will need a "hired girl." Zeena tells Ethan that she hired a girl when she was in Bettsbridge who will be arriving on the train the next afternoon and that Mattie will have to leave so the new girl can have Mattie's bedroom. Ethan is angry, but realizes that Zeena will have her way. He tells Mattie that she will have to leave and he kisses her for the first time. Zeena comes into the kitchen furious because she has found her broken red pickle dish.

Ethan wants to go away with Mattie, but can't leave Zeena destitute. He understands that he is Zeena's prisoner. In the morning, Ethan again goes to visit Mr. Hale to ask for advance payment on lumber, and on his way, stops to speak to Mrs. Hale, who empathizes with him. He realizes that he can't take advantage of the Hales' understanding and returns home. Daniel Byrne, a neighbor, takes Mattie's trunk to the train station. Ethan insists that he will take Mattie to the train station himself.

On the way to the train station, Ethan takes Mattie to Shadow Pond where they first fell in love with each other. At the top of School House Hill, they find a sled and go sledding, successfully swerving, just missing the elm tree at the bottom of the hill. Before taking the sled down the hill again, Mattie tells Ethan that she would sooner die than to live without him. They agree that death would be better than living apart. With the intention of committing suicide, Mattie and Ethan head straight for the elm tree at the bottom of the hill. The suicide attempt fails. Mattie is taken to Mrs. Ned Hale's house to be cared for after the "smash-up" and Ethan is taken to the minister's house. Ethan and Mattie are taken to the Frome farmhouse when they are physically able and are cared for by Zeena. Despite injuries from the smash-up, including a permanent limp, Ethan manages to support the three of them by resuming working on the farm and in the sawmill.

When The Narrator stays overnight at the Frome farm, over twenty years after the smash-up, he is surprised to find that Mattie—crippled by the accident—complains incessantly. In fact, because the women are now so much alike, he has difficulty distinguishing them.

List of Characters

Ethan Frome A long-time resident of Starkfield. He is a thoughtful, sensitive, and extremely unhappy man. Ethan barely supports himself, his wife (Zeena), and his wife's cousin (Mattie) working his farm and operating a sawmill. A sledding accident with Mattie, which was an attempted suicide, results in his physical disability.

Zenobia Frome (Zeena)   Ethan's wife and Mattie's cousin. She is a hypochondriac, constantly suffering from a variety of physical ailments. She is a cold, unhappy, domineering woman who whines and complains incessantly. After Ethan and Mattie's sledding accident, she cares for them and runs the household.

Mattie (Matt) Silver   Zeena's cousin. She joins the Frome household to work as a housekeeper and aide to Zeena. She is a sensitive, cheerful, and understanding person who falls in love with Ethan. After the sledding accident with Ethan, she becomes completely handicapped and as ill-tempered as Zeena.

The Narrator   An engineer working on a job at the power-house at Corbury Junction. He rents a room in Starkfield from Mrs. Ned Hale, and hires Ethan Frome to transport him to and from the train station. The Narrator relates the "frame story" (the prologue and epilogue).

Harmon Gow   A retired stagecoach driver and resident of Starkfield. He provides The Narrator with information about Ethan Frome's life.

Mrs. Ned Hale (Ruth Varnum)   A middle-aged widow. She lives with her mother in the family mansion. Mrs. Hale had been a close friend to Mattie before the sledding accident. She visits Mattie and Zeena twice a year. She talks to The Narrator about Ethan, Zeena, and Mattie.

Andrew Hale   Ned Hale's father. He owns a construction company in Starkfield. He gives the appearance of having money although he is usually behind on his bills. Ethan asks him for a fifty-dollar advance on a load of lumber and he refuses.

Ned Hale   Andrew Hale's oldest son. He marries Ruth Varnum, but is dead by the time The Narrator comes to town.

Mrs. Andrew Hale   Andrew Hale's wife and Ned Hale's mother. She sympathizes with Ethan about how difficult his life has been.

Denis Eady   A wealthy Irishman who inherited his father's grocery store. He is also the proprietor of a livery stable in Starkfield. He courts Mattie.

Jotham Powell   A hired hand at the Frome farm.

Widow Homan   Storeowner. She sells glue to Ethan.

Aunt Martha Pierce   Zeena's aunt. When Zeena goes to Bettsbridge to see Dr. Buck, she stays with Aunt Martha.

Dr. Buck   The doctor Zeena sees in Bettsbridge. He tells her that she has "complications" and advises her not to do any housework.

Aunt Philura Maple   Zeena's aunt. The red glass pickle dish was her wedding present to Ethan and Zeena.

Daniel Byrne   The Fromes' neighbor. He takes Mattie's trunk to the train station.

Character Map

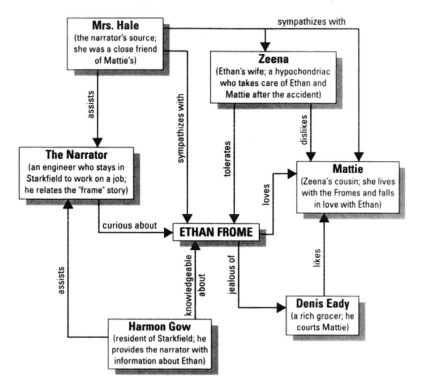

Mrs. Hale
(the narrator's source; she was a close friend of Mattie's)

sympathizes with

Zeena
(Ethan's wife; a hypochondriac who takes care of Ethan and Mattie after the accident)

assists

sympathizes with

tolerates

dislikes

The Narrator
(an engineer who stays in Starkfield to work on a job; he relates the "frame" story)

Mattie
(Zeena's cousin; she lives with the Fromes and falls in love with Ethan)

loves

curious about

ETHAN FROME

assists

knowledgeable about

jealous of

likes

Harmon Gow
(resident of Starkfield; he provides the narrator with information about Ethan)

Denis Eady
(a rich grocer; he courts Mattie)

CRITICAL COMMENTARIES

Prologue

Summary

The Narrator relates the prologue from his point of view. An engineer on temporary assignment for a power company in Corbury Junction, he's staying at Mrs. Ned Hale's in Starkfield. A strike delays his work, giving him an opportunity to observe the citizens of Starkfield, and Ethan Frome in particular.

The Narrator notices Ethan Frome at the post office and is struck by the spectacle of a strong man crippled by physical and mental pain and despair. Upon inquiry among the townspeople, he learns that Ethan is the victim of a "smash-up." His curiosity whetted, The Narrator questions his landlady and Harmon Gow about Ethan's character and his accident, but they do not satisfy The Narrator's desire to know more about Ethan.

The Narrator had been using Denis Eady's horses to get to Corbury Flats to catch the train to the Junction, but all of Eady's horses suddenly become ill. The Narrator acts on a suggestion made by Gow and employs Ethan as a driver. On a trip back to Starkfield with Ethan, a terrible snowstorm causes Ethan to give The Narrator a night's shelter at his farmhouse. When The Narrator walks into the farmhouse he hears a woman's monotonous voice complaining nonstop. The night at the Ethan farm furnishes The Narrator with enough information to put together his vision of Ethan's tragedy.

Commentary

In the prologue, Wharton sets the frame for the main story. The prologue (and epilogue) take place some twenty years after the events of the main story and are written in the first person. The Narrator (who is nameless) tells about how he pieced together the story of Ethan Frome from personal observation and from fragments of the story told to him by townspeople. The prologue not only introduces The Narrator, but also describes Starkfield and the winter setting, inhabitants of Starkfield, and provokes curiosity about the tragedy experienced by Ethan Frome.

According to The Narrator, Ethan constitutes the remains of a once powerful and sensitive man, now bound and frustrated by the crippling effects of a sledding accident. Even though Ethan is only fifty-two years old, he looks as though he is "dead and in hell." Wharton builds suspense when she reveals that The Narrator is also intrigued by the look of incredible suffering and despair that he sees in an unguarded moment on Ethan's face. Wharton provokes curiosity about the tragedy that has robbed Ethan of his life.

Wharton provides minimal information about Ethan. Harmon Gow shares the sad history of the deaths of Ethan's parents and of Zeena's sicknesses, and he adds the comment that "most of the smart ones get away," implying that Ethan was smart, but unfortunately was unable to leave Starkfield.

Theme

The themes of silence and isolation are introduced by the author. The Narrator is impressed with Ethan's solitude and apparent withdrawal into a protective shell. Ethan gives the postman a "silent nod" and would "listen quietly." He responds briefly, in a low tone, when spoken to by one of the townspeople.

Character Insight

Gradually, more of Ethan's character emerges, especially after The Narrator has talked with Ethan during the trips to Corbury Flats. Ethan's intelligence is confirmed for The Narrator through Ethan's interest in a book of popular science, and a parallel between Ethan and The Narrator is established when they reveal that they have both been on engineering trips to Florida. Wharton implies that The Narrator is the kind of man Ethan might have become if he had not become trapped in his marriage. Ethan did the right thing according to the accepted rules of society by caring for his wife; however, it wasn't the right thing for him. Ethan pays the price by never achieving his potential. According to The Narrator, Ethan lives in a "depth of moral isolation."

Literary Device

The most important use of symbolism in the novel is the winter setting, which is first described in the prologue and carried throughout the main story. Harmon Gow's assessment of Ethan early in the prologue is that he has endured too many Starkfield winters. From that point on, winter presides over the tragedy in all its manifestations of snow, ice, wind, cold, darkness, and death. The Narrator speculates that the winters in Ethan's past must have contributed to his current silence and isolation.

**Style &
Language**

Wharton uses battle imagery to describe the way winter conquers Starkfield. The Narrator mentions "the wild cavalry of March winds" and he understood "why Starkfield emerged from its six months' siege like a starved garrison capitulating without quarter." The winter season is predominant: Ethan's memory of his trip to Florida seems to be covered with snow. Even the name of the town, "Starkfield," is significant as a symbolic summation of the moral landscape of the novel. It implies the devastating and isolating effects of the harsh winters on the land and the men who work the land.

The conclusion is that the ravages of winter destroy both man's will to survive and the buildings he constructs to shield him from his environment. The "exanimate," or lifeless, remains of Ethan's sawmill are an example. The Narrator comments on the landscape that also suggests the debilitating effects of winter: the "starved apple-trees writhing over a hillside" suggests the barren land that starves men rather than feeds them. The dead vine on the front porch of Fromes' farmhouse is symbolic of the dead and dying spirits that inhabit the house and its adjacent graveyard. And as The Narrator observes, Fromes' farmhouse "shivers" in the cold and looks "forlorn." After his important description of the "L" shape of the house—"the long deep-roofed adjunct usually built at right angles to the main house, and connecting it, by way of storerooms and tool-house, with the wood-shed and cow-barn"—The Narrator perceives that the farmhouse is symbolic of Ethan himself. The house's function appears to be a place of confinement and isolation for its inhabitants.

Wharton easily changes the focus from The Narrator's first impressions to the dramatic action of the journey taken by Ethan and The Narrator in the snowstorm. It is ironic that a blinding snowstorm forces The Narrator to take shelter in the Frome farmhouse—it opens his eyes to Ethan's story. Thus, the breaking off of the narration just before the door opens increases the suspense and prepares the reader for The Narrator entering the farmhouse in the culmination of the tragedy in the epilogue.

Glossary

(Here and in the following chapters, difficult words and phrases, as well as allusions and historical references, are explained.)

colonnade   a series of columns set at regular intervals, usually supporting a roof or series of arches

pulled me up sharp   caused a person to take notice

chronicle   a narrative; history

mien   a way of carrying and conducting oneself; manner

taciturnity   the fact or condition of being almost always silent, uncommunicative, or not inclined to talk

wust   worst

touch a hundred   turn one hundred years old

chafed   annoyed; irritated

beleaguered   beset, as with difficulties; harassed

portico   a porch or covered walk, consisting of a roof supported by columns, often at the entrance or across the front of a building; colonnade

flagged   made of flagstone, as a walkway or path

innocuous   that which does not injure or harm

reticent   habitually silent or uncommunicative; disinclined to speak readily; reserved; taciturn

oracle   a person of great knowledge or wisdom

inter   into

grit   stubborn courage; brave perseverance; pluck

fust   first

got a kick   was kicked in the head

incarnation   any person or thing serving as the type or embodiment of a quality or concept (the *incarnation* of courage)

sentient   of, having, or capable of feeling or perception; conscious

snowed under   forgotten

unseal his lips   encourage to talk

exanimate   without animation; spiritless; inert

querulously   in a manner inclined to find fault; complainingly

provocation   something that provokes; especially, a cause of resentment or irritation; incitement

Chapters 1–2

Summary

As Chapter 1 begins, Ethan is going into town to walk Mattie Silver home from a dance at the church. Instead of going into the church, Ethan hides in the shadows near a window and watches Mattie dance with Denis Eady. His jealousy prompts Ethan to recall some of the qualities that make Mattie precious to him. He also acknowledges his fear that Mattie has no real affection for him and that Zeena will uncover his growing love for Mattie. This train of thought is triggered by the sight of Mattie treating Eady to some of the mannerisms and affectations that Ethan thought she reserved for him alone. Ethan thinks about Zeena's "sickly" nature and suspects that she feigns part of her illness. He remembers the morning when Zeena observed him shaving and he realized that Zeena is aware of everything that goes on around her—in spite of her illnesses.

Feeling shy because of his recollections of Zeena and his reaction to Mattie's attentions to Eady, Ethan decides to test Mattie and see if she will ride home with Eady. Mattie refuses Eady and as she goes off alone to walk home, Ethan catches up with her. He feels happy by what he perceives as her choice of him over Eady. The couple stops for a moment above the Corbury hill as Mattie tells Ethan about Ned Hale and Ruth Varnum's brush with death as their sled almost hit the elm tree on its downhill run.

Because Ethan is insecure, he intimates that Mattie will be leaving the Fromes' house to marry Eady. Mattie interprets Ethan's comment about the fact that she might want to marry Eady to mean that Zeena wants her gone. She apologizes for her inadequacies as a houseworker, and asks Ethan to clarify what he means. Ethan, however, is unable to communicate his true feelings.

Approaching the farmhouse, Ethan is reassured that Mattie will not marry Eady. He walks arm in arm with her and when she stumbles, uses the opportunity to put his arm around her. When they reach the back door, they cannot find the door key that Zeena always leaves for them. As Ethan searches for the key in the snow, he sees light under the door and Zeena opens it. She hadn't put the key out because she was up; she felt "so mean" she could not sleep. After scolding Ethan and Mattie about the snow on their boots, Zeena starts to go off to bed; Ethan does not want to follow her upstairs to their bedroom but thinks he sees Mattie blink him a warning, so he gives in to his wife and goes to bed.

Commentary

Chapter 1 begins the main story of *Ethan Frome*, which takes place about twenty-four years earlier than the prologue and epilogue and describes the three and a half days before and including the "smash-up" (Mattie and Ethan's sledding accident). Wharton shifts the point of view in this chapter from the first person to the limited omniscient point of view. The *limited omniscient point of view* allows Wharton to relate the thoughts and feelings of only one character. In *Ethan Frome*, Wharton relates the thoughts and feelings of Ethan.

As the story opens, Wharton continues the imagery and symbolism of the winter setting in Starkfield. The first paragraph describes the winter night when Ethan walks into town to meet Mattie at the church. It is windy, and there is two feet of snow on the ground; the stars shine like icicles and Orion seems to be a "cold fire." ("Cold fire" is an *oxymoron*—a figure of speech in which terms with opposite meanings are combined.) Wharton's intention is to emphasize the bitterness and hardness of the winter by describing a star in a "sky of iron." On the walk home, when Mattie assures Ethan that she does not want to leave the Frome household, "the iron heavens seemed to melt and rain down sweetness."

Wharton uses imagery associated with winter to characterize Zeena, and imagery of spring and summer to represent Mattie. When Ethan reaches the church, he stays in "pure and frosty darkness," analogous to the silence and isolation he experiences and in opposition to the happy sociability of the interior of the church which he sees in "a mist of heat" caused by the "volcanic fires" from the stove in the room. Ethan feels that Mattie's effect on him is like "the lighting of a fire on a cold hearth." Her face seems to him "like a window that has caught the sunset." On their walk home from the church, when Ethan reveals to Mattie that he had been hiding while she talked to Eady, "her wonder and his laughter ran together like spring rills in a thaw." Mattie's changes in mood seem to Ethan to be like "the flit of a bird in the branches." And when he finally gets up the courage to put his arm around Mattie, he feels that walking with her is like "floating on a summer stream."

Literary Device

In contrast to the warm, summer imagery associated with Mattie is the imagery that represents the cold, isolation, and death of spirit inherent during the winter months and apparently present in the Frome farmhouse. Returning home from the church, Ethan and Mattie see farmhouses that seem to be "mute and cold as a gravestone." They see the dead cucumber vine at the Frome farmhouse that looks "like the crape streamer tied to the door for death." And, the kitchen has "the deadly chill of a vault after the dry cold of the night." These images are related to the fascination that Ethan finds in his family graveyard, and they are also appropriate to the living death that Ethan and Mattie experience after their accident. Their lives become cold and dead and Ethan experiences more intense silence and isolation than he did before Mattie came into his life.

Character Insight

Wharton reveals important aspects of Ethan's character and introduces readers to Zeena and Mattie. Ethan is an intelligent man; he spent time at a technological college, but had to quit and return home when his father died. His schooling "made him aware of huge cloudy meanings behind the daily face of things." Ethan learned that he has the freedom to think and his thoughts have become his world and his life. He retreats into his thoughts to avoid the pain of reality. Ethan's thoughts are sometimes imprecise and irrational—they too often consist of illusions or half-truths rather than clear intuitions or reasoned conclusions. Ethan constantly tries to analyze and control what is happening in the present and dreams and wonders about the future.

Wharton introduces Mattie through Ethan's thoughts while he is waiting for her by the church window. Mattie is first identified as Zeena's cousin, who has come to Starkfield as a household helper, and is allowed to go into town from the farm to attend social activities. According to Ethan's perspective, Mattie is the happy opposite of the cold and complaining Zeena. The tense silence and isolation that dominates Ethan's marriage to Zeena is not present in his relationship with Mattie. In contrast to Zeena, Mattie has a sensitive nature and is able to communicate with Ethan and Ethan with her. Mattie shares his appreciation of natural beauty. When Mattie exclaims that a sunset looks "just as if it was painted," Ethan feels as though he has found his soul mate. As a result of his secret feelings for Mattie, Ethan often tries to escape the reality of his marriage by indulging in self-illusion, or fantasies.

As Ethan continues to watch Mattie from outside the window of the church, he feels fearful because Eady is flirting with Mattie. The fears that Ethan forces on himself are an example of his use of self-illusion as an escape. In his mind, Mattie's smiles and gestures have been just for him. Ethan's unhappy thoughts turn to thoughts of Zeena.

Wharton characterizes Zeena as "sickly." Ethan is suspicious of how sick she really is, suspecting that she may be feigning part of her illness. Ethan's memory of the morning when Zeena watched him shaving serves to foreshadow her character and physical appearance before her dramatic appearance on the Frome back porch: she has a gray complexion, high cheek bones, and a drawling voice. Zeena's vindictive nature casts a pall of dominance over Ethan and Mattie throughout the novel.

As Mattie and Ethan walk home, Wharton emphasizes the difficulty Ethan has in communicating with Mattie. He is unable to express his affection in words or action. When provided the opportunity to reveal his feelings to Mattie, he can only say, "Come along." The isolation and silence that Ethan experiences (a result of the lack of communication in his marriage), have become barriers that inhibit him. Because Ethan is incapable of telling Mattie that he loves her, he "attach(es) a fantastic importance to every change in her look and tone." He needs her approval to fuel his romantic illusions. Ethan's insecurity causes him to intimate that her rejection of him is because she intends to marry Eady and leave the Frome farm.

Ethan's love for Mattie as yet remains one-sided and is fed on illusion. The closest Ethan can come to telling Mattie how he feels is to pull her to him and whisper that they will always be together. Ironically, they are passing the graveyard as he pronounces these words, and Wharton foreshadows their death in life.

Mattie tells Ethan about Ned Hale and Ruth Varnum's brush with death when their sled almost hit the elm tree as it was going downhill. This couple serves as a symbol for Ethan and Mattie of the happiness that they might have, and Ethan bases some of his illusions about himself and Mattie on Ned and Ruth's actions. This description of Ned and Ruth's near accident on Corbury hill, plus an earlier mention of Corbury hill and sledding, foreshadows Ethan and Mattie's smash-up.

As Ethan and Mattie near the farmhouse, Ethan sees the dead cucumber vine that reminds him of a funeral crape. He half wishes it were there for Zeena: Ethan subconsciously wishes she were dead. He has the same thought when he cannot find the back-door key and thinks that tramps might have broken into the house.

Wharton hints at Zeena's sickness and disagreeable nature and describes various unattractive physical characteristics. When Zeena opens the back door, Ethan really sees her for the first time. Wharton's description of Zeena emphasizes the hard and cold nature of the woman. She is "tall and angular," with a "flat breast," "puckered throat," and "projecting wrist." She is the ugly reality from which Ethan is trying to escape in his dreams of Mattie.

Zeena has felt "so mean" she could not sleep. In colloquial usage the words denote that she felt ill, but there is an ironic connotation of Zeena's vindictiveness intended as well. It appears that Zeena wields some kind of power over Ethan. When Ethan realized, years ago, that he could not communicate with her, he became acquiescent. In this situation, he gives in to his wife, and with Mattie's warning look, goes to bed.

Glossary

Dipper   the Big Dipper; a dipper-shaped group of stars in the constellation Ursa Major

Orion   an equatorial constellation between Taurus and Lepus, containing the bright stars Rigel and Betelgeuse

peristyle   a row of columns forming an enclosure or supporting a roof

declivity   a downward slope or sloping, as of a hill

vexed   to give trouble to, esp. in a petty or nagging way; disturb, annoy, irritate, etc.

effrontery   unashamed boldness; impudence; audacity; presumption

revelry   reveling; noisy merrymaking; boisterous festivity

Aldebaran   a galactic cluster

Pleiades   a galactic cluster in the constellation Taurus

fatuity stupidity, especially complacent stupidity; smug foolishness

self-effacement the practice of keeping oneself in the background and minimizing one's own actions; modest, retiring behavior

roan of a solid color, as reddish-brown, brown, black, etc., with a thick sprinkling of white hairs; said chiefly of horses

rills little brooks; rivulets

crape streamer a piece of black crepe as a sign of mourning, often worn as a band around the arm

repugnant contradictory; inconsistent; offering resistance; opposed; antagonistic

Chapters 3–5

Summary

The next morning, Ethan is out early hauling lumber. He thinks about the previous night when he lay awake until the light in Mattie's room went out. He remembered when Mattie first came to stay with the Fromes. She had not had any place else to go. Her father, Zeena's cousin, squandered money before dying unexpectedly, and shortly thereafter, Mattie's mother died, leaving her destitute. Because family members lost money by trusting Mattie's father with it, they punished Mattie by refusing to help her. Zeena needed household help because of her illness, so Mattie arrived in Starkfield to work for Zeena.

At first, Zeena found fault with everything Mattie did; however, over time, the situation became less tense. After the warning look that Mattie had given Ethan the previous night, Ethan felt it was necessary to leave his work and return home to be sure there was no trouble between Mattie and Zeena.

Ethan was surprised to see Zeena sitting in the kitchen with her suitcase. She announced that she was going to Bettsbridge to see a doctor and would be staying with her aunt, Martha Pierce. The first thought that came to Ethan's mind was that he would be alone with Mattie for one full night. Because he didn't want to drive Zeena to the Junction, he lied to her, saying he needed to pick up money from Andrew Hale but that Jotham Powell would drive her.

After Zeena leaves, Ethan leaves the house also to take his load of lumber to Andrew Hale. On the way he thinks about his past—the death of his father, the responsibility of running the farm and mill, his mother's silence and ultimate death, and his marriage to Zeena after she had cared for his mother. The couple wanted to move away from Starkfield, but Ethan couldn't find a buyer for the farm and mill and he realized that Zeena needed to stay in Starkfield where she was well known (if only for being "sickly"). Zeena soon became silent also and communication between the couple came to a halt.

After delivering lumber to Andrew Hale and asking for payment (which he doesn't get), Ethan takes care of other business in town and heads home. When he gets home, the back door is locked. He calls for Mattie and she opens the door, standing exactly as Zeena stood the night before.

Mattie set the dinner table special for Ethan, using Zeena's cherished red pickle dish. During the course of their meal, the cat knocks the dish and it falls on the floor and breaks. Mattie is quite upset, but Ethan pieces the dish together, puts it on the shelf, and promises to glue it together the next day. Mattie clears the table and they sit down near the fire. Mattie and Ethan talk comfortably with each other while Mattie sews. When the cat jumps from Zeena's chair, they are reminded of Zeena's return. They take care of their nightly chores and go to bed.

Commentary

In anticipation of Ethan and Mattie's evening together during Zeena's trip to Bettsbridge, Wharton has Ethan recall Mattie's background and the details of how she came to live with the Fromes. If Mattie's accomplishments such as making candy and trimming hats seem frivolous in the face of the hard work she is required to do for Zeena, these abilities represent a youthful and happy personality which is able to entertain itself with frivolity instead of moping in self-pity about imagined ills as Zeena does.

Mattie is in most ways the opposite of Zeena; Mattie is happy, healthy, pretty and young, while Zeena is unhappy, sickly, ugly, and seven years older than Ethan. In Mattie, Wharton creates a character who is naturally appealing while presenting Zeena as an unlikable and cold woman. Zeena is whining and petulant and her presence must be endured.

When describing Zeena sitting at the table, Wharton uses bleak and cold imagery. Zeena sits in "the pale light reflected from the banks of snow," which makes "her face look more than usually drawn and bloodless," and makes her other unattractive features more apparent.

Ethan's first thought about Zeena's trip is that such trips have cost him a lot of money in the past, and the remedies have not had a positive effect on Zeena's illness. He disregards these unpleasant recollections when he realizes that he will be able to spend the night alone with Mattie. Ethan's fears that Zeena may suspect his love for Mattie are allayed when he realizes that Zeena was indeed feeling ill the previous night. Ethan, who is normally rather honest, comes up with a story to tell Zeena about why he can't drive her to the train station.

The story Ethan comes up with (going into town to be paid for lumber) is acceptable to Zeena. He realizes that it was not a good idea to let Zeena know that he has any money before she went on one of her expensive journeys to doctors. Such considerations are quickly put aside, as Ethan returns to thoughts about the evening with Mattie. The lie that he told Zeena will come back to haunt him because Zeena later justifies hiring a girl to replace Mattie based on the money Ethan was supposed to be getting.

After Zeena leaves with Jotham Powell, the kitchen seems more comfortable and inviting because Mattie and Ethan are alone. Ethan goes to town, his mind is busy conjuring up pictures of what the evening with Mattie will be like. It is important to note that Ethan visualizes nothing illicit or immoral; all he hopes for is an evening of companionship before the fire.

Theme

Ethan's thoughts about the evening prompt him to think about the silence that has been part of his life since his college days. The theme of silence is discussed with reference to Ethan's past. Some of the symptoms of the silence surrounding Ethan were his inability to communicate with Zeena and his halting efforts to say something significant to Mattie. The silence imposed by his marriage to Zeena is one of the causes of Ethan's need for illusion. Illusion in turn reinforces the silence by helping Ethan avoid communication by fantasizing. Wharton reveals the background of Ethan's marriage to Zeena is revealed so the evening with Mattie in which silence is partially conquered will be prepared for. Wharton reveals the depth of isolation that Ethan experiences in his mind as a result of living in a silent house with a silent woman.

Character Insight

Because Ethan couldn't bear to be alone, he married Zeena (who had been living with him, caring for his mother). He now wonders whether or not he would have married Zeena if it had been spring instead of winter. Ethan realizes that his fear of loneliness rather than love for Zeena prompted their marriage. After the death of his father, Ethan had the responsibility of the farm and mill, leaving him little time for establishing relationships with villagers. When his mother stopped talking, Ethan felt as though the silence would drive him mad.

After delivering lumber to Andrew Hale and asking Hale for money (which Ethan is refused), Ethan drives home and passes the family cemetery where the family tombstone of Ethan and Endurance Frome proclaims that they shared fifty years of wedded bliss. The epitaph seems ironic to Ethan. Recently reminded of seven years' endurance of Zeena, he wonders what people might someday say about the two of them. More important as a parallel to the previous night's action (when he walked by the cemetery with Mattie), Ethan's thoughts show that he now seriously does consider himself married to Zeena, and that he briefly realizes his thoughts of being buried in the cemetery with Mattie were fantasy. The headstone is also ironic because, in the end, it is Zeena who must forego her illnesses and prove herself in the role of "endurance" in anything but peaceful circumstances as she ministers for years to the two crippled victims of the sledding accident.

Style & Language

The events of the night before are paralleled in order to draw attention in a dramatic and climactic moment to the difference between Zeena and Mattie. When Mattie lets Ethan in the locked back door, standing in the same pose that Zeena did the night before, Ethan is struck by the immense difference between the young, warm, and feminine Mattie and his old, cold, and hard wife Zeena.

Character Insight

Wharton structures the events in this way to allow Mattie to demonstrate her feelings for Ethan without oral communication. Mattie shows Ethan how special he is to her by adding a red ribbon to her hair, laughing, and preparing Ethan's favorite foods.

Literary Device

During the meal, Ethan and Mattie are uncomfortable mentioning Zeena's name. Wharton uses the cat as a stand-in for Zeena. Mattie almost trips over the cat, the cat sits in Zeena's chair during the meal, the cat causes the pickle dish to be broken and sits in Zeena's chair near the fire.

Breaking the pickle dish is a climactic event in the novel. Mattie uses the pickle dish, one of Zeena's most cherished wedding presents, for one of Ethan's favorite foods and to set a special table for Ethan. Using the pickle dish is a trespass against Zeena. Neither Ethan nor Mattie want to acknowledge the trespass to Zeena, and to cover up their guilt, Ethan becomes assertive. He deliberately intends to deceive Zeena by gluing the dish back together in order to protect Mattie. This act enables Ethan to feel a sense of masculine dominance, a feeling he has never experienced with Zeena.

Literary Device

After the meal, Ethan and Mattie communicate easily with each other, enjoying the companionship of the other. Ethan allows himself to imagine that Mattie is his wife and this particular night is typical for them. He talks of going coasting and enjoys the sense of masculine superiority by trying to make Mattie admit she would be afraid. They talk again about sledding, the reference to coasting foreshadowing their smash-up. Ethan and Mattie also talk about Zeena and the fact that she is dissatisfied with Mattie's abilities to perform the household chores. They both agree that Zeena is unpredictable. Wharton foreshadows Zeena's decision to fire Mattie and get a new girl to do the housework.

Wharton associates the imagery of warmth, summer, and natural life with Mattie: her face seems "like a wheat field under a summer breeze"; her pronunciation of the word "married" seems to invoke "a rustling covert leading to enchanted glades"; and the action of her hands over her sewing resembles birds building their nests.

After being startled once again by the cat jumping out of Zeena's rocker, Ethan realizes that the evening has been much like a dream. He and Mattie have done their best to avoid reality and Ethan feels weary and defeated. Ethan kisses the material that Mattie is sewing as a gesture of the intimacy of the evening. They go off to bed, realizing that they each have feelings for the other. It is the first moment that Ethan and Mattie convey their true feelings to one another.

Glossary

scintillating   sparkling intellectually; brilliant and witty

draughts   deep breaths

imperceptible   not plain or distinct to the senses or the mind; especially, so slight, gradual, subtle, etc.; as not to be easily perceived

merino   fine wool, originally from Spain

undulations   wavy, curving forms or outlines, especially in a series

bandbox   a light, round box to hold hats, collars, etc.

flux   to flow or stream out

spruce   dress in a neat and trim in a smart, dapper way

marrow   the innermost, essential, or choicest part; pith

cessation   a ceasing, or stopping, either forever or for some time

convivial   fond of eating, drinking, and good company; sociable; jovial

taciturnity   the fact or condition of being almost always silent or uncommunicative, or not inclined to talk

precedent   that precedes; preceding

conjoined   joined together; united; combined

rent   a hole or gap made by rending or tearing, as a torn place in cloth, a fissure in the earth, etc.

kindled   caused to light up; made bright

indolent   disliking or avoiding work; idle; lazy

wainscot   a wood lining or paneling on the walls of a room; sometimes, specifically, such paneling on the lower part of the walls only

spectral   of, having the nature of, or like a specter; phantom; ghostly

Chapters 6–7

Summary

The next morning, Ethan is feeling quite happy. He has a vision of what life could be like with Mattie. Ethan leaves for work and tells Mattie that he will be home for dinner. During the morning, everything that can possibly go wrong, does. Delayed by problems, Ethan decides to go to Starkfield to get the glue to mend Zeena's red dish after his mid-day meal. He wants to get home and mend the dish before Zeena's return. In the village, Ethan is further delayed when the first shop he tries doesn't have what he needs. He goes to Mrs. Homan's shop, purchases her last bottle of glue, and returns home as fast as possible.

When Ethan arrives home, he shows Mattie the glue and intends to repair the dish but Mattie stops him. Zeena is home and is upstairs in her room. Ethan assures Mattie that he will mend the dish during the night so Zeena will not find out it was broken.

Ethan invites Jotham Powell to supper, but to Ethan's surprise, Jotham declines the invitation. Ethan thought Jotham would be a restraining influence during the meal. Ethan considers Jotham's refusal to be a warning of Zeena's mood. When he returns to the house, Mattie's preparations for supper make it seem as warm and hospitable as the evening before.

Ethan goes to the bedroom to see Zeena. Zeena informs Ethan that she has "complications": She is seriously sick. Ethan feels compassion for her believing that she may have a serious illness. Zeena informs Ethan that Dr. Buck has prescribed that she do no more work around the house and that she has hired a new girl to come and assume the household duties. Ethan is so shocked by the blow to his pocketbook that he does not think of the implications for Mattie. His anger is roused but in the argument that follows he is forced to admit lamely that he was unable to get the money from Andrew Hale. He realizes he has been caught in a lie.

Zeena tells Ethan that the new girl will be arriving the next day and that Mattie will have to leave at once. Ethan leaves the bedroom and finds Mattie downstairs in the kitchen. Without explaining why, Ethan embraces and kisses Mattie, caught up in love for her and hate for

Zeena. Ethan breaks the news to Mattie. When he considers what her plight will be when thrown on the mercies of the outside world, Ethan is moved to swear that he will reverse Zeena's decision. He stops speaking in mid-sentence when Zeena enters the kitchen. Zeena sits down at the table, eats, and converses about physical problems among her friends and relatives.

After eating, Zeena complains that the meal has given her indigestion. She goes to get her heartburn medicine and discovers the broken red pickle dish. Zeena returns to the kitchen demanding to know how her dish broke. Mattie tells her the truth and Zeena scolds her. Zeena leaves the room carrying the pickle dish as if it were a dead body. This incident gives Zeena more justification for sending Mattie away.

Commentary

Ethan's happiness after his evening with Mattie is a product of his self-deception. He still has not considered the implications of his love for Mattie. He fantasizes about the evening and still cannot bring himself to verbalize his feelings to Mattie. He sits and watches her do dishes. The imagery Wharton associates with Mattie continues to be that of warmth, life, and the spring and summer. The steam from the hot water has made Mattie's hair especially curly so that it resembles the "traveller's joy," a climbing vine also appropriately known as virgin's bowers.

When Ethan returns to the farmhouse with the glue, Mattie's preparations for supper make the house seem as warm and hospitable as the previous evening. Dramatic irony is evident. Ethan and Mattie momentarily remember the happiness they shared the night before; however, their memories are a prelude to the anxiety and grief that is to come. Zeena's wish to have Mattie out of the house will destroy the false sense of security that Ethan has felt and will break the illusion that he and Mattie will be able to endure Zeena together.

Ethan's confrontation with Zeena occurs in their bedroom; a room ruled by Zeena. It is important to note that in the bedroom Zeena has previously asserted herself over Ethan (such as when she made a derisive comment to him about shaving every morning since Mattie's arrival) and that Ethan thinks best when he is outside in the cold air. The imagery that Wharton associates with the confrontation between Ethan and Zeena is that of darkness. She uses words such as "dark," "obscurity," "dim," "twilight," and "darkness."

Zeena is quite cunning about the way she asserts her dominance over Ethan. She tells him about her "complications," eliciting his compassion for her, then she resolutely informs him that she has hired a girl to do the housework. Ethan (who didn't get the money from Andrew Hale) feels guilty about the lie he'd told Zeena, and Zeena tells him they will be saving money on Mattie's keep.

Character Insight

Zeena has conquered Ethan and he knows it. He attempts to change Zeena's mind by urging her to do the "right thing" (after all, Mattie is her relation). Zeena's authority prevails and she tells him the new girl will be arriving the next day. Ethan realizes his powerlessness and weakness. He finally sees clearly that Zeena controls him and what happens in the house. He sees her as an "alien presence," "an evil energy." Wharton points out Ethan's awareness that he is entrapped in a loveless marriage. She alludes to the notion that Ethan will not violate his marriage vows (the rules of society). Ethan becomes so angry with Zeena that he wants to strike her, but he backs down and leaves the room. Ethan knows that Zeena has complete control over him.

Style & Language

When Ethan goes downstairs to eat dinner and reveal to Mattie that there is trouble, Wharton again makes use of imagery. Mattie's fear causes her eyelashes to beat against Ethan's cheek "like netted butterflies." Ethan speaks to Mattie "as if he saw her drowning in a dream." Their conversation has the effect of "a torch of warning" in a "black landscape." Ethan feels as intoxicated as when kissing Mattie, but at the same time he is "dying of thirst for her lips." These images used by Wharton are suggestive of captivity and death. The imagery is foreboding and foreshadows the tragedy that befalls Ethan and Mattie.

As Ethan is in the midst of his manly defense of Mattie, Zeena enters the kitchen. Her entrance causes Ethan to stop speaking in midsentence: Zeena's dominance over Ethan is complete. Even after demonstrating his love for Mattie, he can not defend her in front of Zeena. Zeena sits at the table triumphant, smiling and flaunting her power over Mattie and Ethan. When she leaves the room to get her stomach medicine, Mattie and Ethan look at each other and "the warm still kitchen looked as peaceful as the night before." Ironically, the moment is the calm before the storm.

Zeena finds the broken pickle dish and is visibly angered. Ethan once again becomes powerless when Zeena realizes he lied about the dish to protect Mattie. Ethan is unable to challenge Zeena, even to stand up for Mattie. Wharton foreshadows the smash-up as she describes Zeena carrying the pieces of broken pickle dish "as if she carried a dead body." Ironically, Zeena's concern will soon have to be for the broken bodies of Ethan and Mattie.

Glossary

milden   to make or become mild

sledge   a sled or sleigh for carrying loads over ice, snow, etc.

deigned   condescended to do something thought to be slightly beneath one's dignity

aver   to declare to be true; state positively; affirm

consecrated   caused to be revered or honored

felicitous   used or expressed in a way suitable to the occasion; aptly chosen; appropriate; apt

extry   extra

foist   to get (a thing) accepted, sold, etc. by fraud, deception, etc.; palm off

grudged   felt a strong, continued sense of hostility or ill will against someone over a real or fancied grievance

afore   before

inexorable   that cannot be moved or influenced by persuasion or entreaty; unrelenting

antipathy   strong or deep-rooted dislike; aversion

smote   defeated, punished, destroyed, or killed

compunction   a sharp feeling of uneasiness brought on by a sense of guilt; remorse

ingratiatingly   so as to make acceptable; especially, so as to bring (oneself) into another's favor or good graces by conscious effort

shan't meddle   won't interfere

rejoined   joined together again; reunited

evocation   an evoking, or calling forth

Chapters 8–9

Summary

That night, after Ethan is sure Zeena is asleep, he goes downstairs to his cold study to think about all that had happened that evening. He has the note that Mattie had written him earlier in the evening telling him not to trouble himself with the situation. The note was the only note Mattie had ever written him, and in a way, it is the first real sign of communication of her affection for him.

Ethan lays down on the sofa and feels something poking his cheek. He realizes it is a cushion Zeena made for him and he throws it across the room. Ethan considers rebelling against Zeena, violating the rules of society, and divorcing her to run away with Mattie. He recalls the story of a man who left his wife by fleeing to the West with his lover and leaving his farm to his wife. Ethan thinks the plan is a good one and begins to write a note of explanation to Zeena. He realizes that money is a problem. He doesn't have money for train fare for himself and Mattie, and Zeena would not be able to get any money from the sale of the farm or mill.

Mattie finds him sleeping in his study the next morning. He gets up and they begin the morning chores. At breakfast, Zeena confirms her decision of the previous night by telling Jotham that Daniel Byrne is going to pick up Mattie's trunk and take it to the train station.

Ethan decides to ask Andrew Hale for the money owed him once again, but on the way he meets Mrs. Hale who is sympathetic towards him. He realizes that he can't ask for the money and must accept the reality of the situation.

While he's home for lunch, Ethan defies Zeena and refuses to allow Jotham to drive Mattie to the train station, insisting that he drive Mattie himself.

Zeena retires to her bedroom, and Mattie and Ethan begin their journey to the train station. Ethan tries to tell Mattie of his wish to run away with her, and she produces the note he'd written the night before that she'd found in his study. They confirm that their imagined love for each other is real.

They arrive at the sledding hill and decide to make good on the plans they had to go sledding together. After they successfully coast down the hill once, they kiss good-bye. Because they don't wish to be separated, ever, they decide to commit suicide by sledding into the elm tree. As they start down the hill and approach the elm tree, Ethan has an ugly vision of Zeena's face that causes him to swerve the sled; but he resumes the course and steers the sled into the elm tree.

As Ethan regains consciousness, his vision returns and he tries to determine if the star he is looking at is Sirius. As his hearing returns, he hears the sound of a small animal calling out in pain. He becomes aware that the sound is coming from under his hand, which is on Mattie's face in the snow. He hears his horse whinny and is reminded that the horse needs to be fed.

Commentary

When Ethan goes to his study and lies down on the sofa, a cushion that Zeena made for him—the only piece of needlework that Zeena had ever done—pokes him in the cheek. Ethan throws the cushion across the room. His action is symbolic of his growing rejection of Zeena. He thinks of going West with Mattie and of escaping from Zeena, but realizes that he is a prisoner of circumstance. Wharton uses the image of captivity to convey Ethan's feeling of despair; "the inexorable facts closed in on him like prison-warders handcuffing a convict," "he was a prisoner for life." Ethan is caught in physical and mental darkness. Wharton contrasts Ethan's gloom with a sudden, mocking illumination of the night sky as the "pure moon" reveals all the natural beauty of the landscape that Ethan associates with Mattie. The moon also foreshadows the sledding accident as Ethan remembers that this is the night when he had promised to take Mattie sledding.

After Mattie finds him and they begin the morning chores, things don't seem so bleak to Ethan. His self-deceptive optimism about Mattie takes over his thoughts, and despite his earlier realization that Zeena's decision is unchangeable, he decides that things are not hopeless and that he can find a way to keep Mattie at home with him.

 At breakfast when Zeena confirms to Jotham that Mattie would definitely be leaving, Ethan's subservience to her is again evident. He does not mention his thoughts or intentions. He fails, once again, to assert himself over his wife.

Again, Ethan feels defeated. His reaction is to rebel against Zeena. He is determined to do something to change the situation. He decides to go to Andrew Hale once again for the money he is owed, but on the way, he meets Mrs. Hale, who is sympathetic towards him. His conscience prevents him from asking for the money. Wharton makes it clear that Ethan is inescapably bound within the segment of society that he inhabits. Part of his tragedy is that his aspirations and dreams would take him beyond the icy world of Starkfield. His fate, however, is to serve out his life chained to a frigid, quarrelsome wife and to the crippled remains of a once beautiful girl. Wharton makes sure that there is no possible alternative of escape in Ethan's mind when he is faced with the decision of whether or not to attempt suicide with Mattie. His conscience forces him to turn away from the Hales and to return to the farm.

After Ethan confronts Zeena and insists that he will drive Mattie to the train station, Wharton does not bring Zeena into the action again. Zeena retires, triumphant, to her bedroom. Wharton begins to build the suspense that leads to the climax of the story.

As Mattie and Ethan begin their ride, Ethan feels almost happy. He takes a route that leads them to Shadow Pond. The name "Shadow" is suggestive of the memories that Ethan and Mattie have of the spot; as well, it connotes the inability that Mattie and Ethan have of really communicating their feelings to each other. The incident in which Ethan found Mattie's locket when they attended a church picnic, soon after Mattie had arrived at the Frome household, is symbolic of the love that he found with it. It is not unreasonable to suppose that the gold trinket represents Mattie's heart. But, at the time it happened, the incident only foreshadowed what might come to pass. Similarly, their return visit to the spot causes Ethan and Mattie to wonder about their love without speaking about it. It is Mattie who realizes that they must give in to the pressures of time and continue on their trip to the station.

Style & Language

The descriptions Wharton provides of the drive to the pond and the pond itself are rich with images of natural beauty, a contrast to the stark and cold images that are characteristic of most of the novel. The couple reminisces about the picnic the previous summer; Mattie sat looking "pretty as a picture in (her) pink hat," there was a "pebbly beach," and they sat together on a tree trunk in the sun.

As time passes, increasing darkness prevails over the imagery as Ethan and Mattie approach their sledding accident. Wharton suggests the mood of the tragic climax and the characters' thoughts of death when she has the darkness come "dropping down like a black veil from the heavy hemlock boughs." The black veil is evocative of a funeral and the hemlock of poison.

The theme of entrapment in a loveless marriage due to the unwillingness to violate the rules of society is again evident. Ethan tells Mattie that he is "tied hand and foot," and "there isn't a thing I can do." Mattie understands that it is not possible to escape from the situation.

Mattie reveals that she has the note Ethan wrote to Zeena the previous night, and his love for her is clear. Mattie and Ethan confirm that their love for each other is indeed real. The revelation is also sad because they must part. The couple first voice their feelings that they'd rather be dead than be apart.

Wharton creates suspense as the couple arrives at the sledding hill and decide to go sledding. After the first ride, Ethan asks Mattie if she was scared of running into the elm tree. The idea of fear signals the mounting pressure of the death wish building in the two lovers. It also foreshadows the accident. As the conversation about fear and the thrilling exaltation of the sled ride have passed, silence, darkness, and cold are emphasized as the couple climbs up the hill. Ethan thinks this will be their last walk together. His thoughts foreshadow not only the coming accident, but also Mattie's future as a cripple.

As the idea of a mutual death gains momentum, Ethan is caught in a frenzy of love for Mattie that blots out his former conscientious thoughts of not leaving Zeena to fend for herself. Ethan is overwhelmed by the knowledge that Mattie loves him. Only the touch of Mattie's cold cheek and the whistle of the approaching train bring him out of his vision.

The idea of mutual suicide is now identified in Ethan's mind as a sort of quest to preserve the love and beauty of his relationship with Mattie. Passion, not reason, dominates his mind; appropriately, the darkness has increased and his usually sharp vision is dimmed, just as his rational faculties are dimmed in the obscurity of passion.

As they coast downhill, the last thing Ethan sees before the tree is a vision of his wife's face, a manifestation of his conception of her as an alien presence. It seems to try to prevent him from attaining the goal of the tree, but he maneuvers around it. The vision is a symbolic reminder that Ethan will never escape Zeena's dominance, and that he will fail tragically in his attempt to carry away in death the beauty and love he found with Mattie.

After the crash into the tree, Wharton describes what Ethan sees and feels; he had wondered briefly what it would be like after death but now he slowly realizes he is still alive. Mattie's beauty has turned into the twisted, ugly reality that Ethan will have to bear for the rest of his life.

The accident results in the destruction of two lives. Wharton does not tell readers that the attempt at death has failed and that Ethan and Mattie are condemned to live out their crippled lives in Starkfield. Instead, readers can sense with Ethan the quiet acceptance of his fate when he thinks that it is time to feed his horse. For Ethan, there is no escape from the silence, isolation, and entrapment.

Glossary

protuberances   parts or things that protrude; projections; bulges; swellings

injunction   an enjoining; bidding; command

lumbago   rheumatic pain in the lumbar region; backache, especially in the lower part of the back

repining   a feeling or expression of unhappiness or discontent; complaint; fretting

mottlings   blotches, streaks, and spots of different colors or shades

boles   tree trunks

facetious   joking or trying to be jocular, especially at an inappropriate time

uncouth   uncultured; crude; boorish

adjured   entreated solemnly; appealed to earnestly

discursively in a manner characterized by wandering from one topic to another or skimming over many apparently unconnected subjects; in a rambling, desultory, or digressive manner

audacity bold courage; daring

lineaments features of the body, usually of the face, especially with regard to its outline

Sirius a binary star in the constellation Canis Major, the brightest star in the sky

Epilogue

Summary

Ethan and The Narrator enter the Frome farmhouse. The complaining voice that The Narrator heard outside the door stops. The Narrator notices the shabby furnishings in the room. The tall woman gets up from her chair to prepare supper and the other woman remains in her chair because she is paralyzed.

Ethan comments on the cold temperature in the room and the woman sitting in the chair complains that her companion fell asleep and had not kept the fire going. Ethan introduces The Narrator to his wife, Zeena, who brings the food to the table, and to Mattie, who sits in the chair complaining incessantly.

The next day, The Narrator tells Mrs. Hale and old Mrs. Varnum that he'd stayed at the Frome house. Mrs. Hale is surprised because she and the doctor are the only visitors usually admitted to the Frome house. Mrs. Hale makes the trip now only about twice a year and she prefers to go when she knows Ethan will not be home because she can sense the terrible pain he feels at being trapped in the farmhouse. Because he'd gained entrance to the house, Mrs. Hale feels as though she can divulge more information about the smash-up to The Narrator.

Mrs. Hale relates that after Ethan and Mattie collided with the elm tree, Mattie was taken to the Varnum house. Mrs. Hale (the former Ruth Varnum) was with her when she regained consciousness. Zeena arrived at Ethan's bedside to care for him and, when Mattie was well enough, took her to the farmhouse and cared for her also. Mattie has lived with the Fromes ever since the accident. Mrs. Hale explains that because of her suffering, Mattie has become as querulous as Zeena. She comments that if Mattie had died at the time of the smash-up, Ethan might have been able to live.

Commentary

Wharton once again shifts the point of view to the first person; The Narrator resumes the story about Ethan Frome that he began in the prologue more than twenty years after the tragedy experienced by Ethan and Mattie. The epilogue is a *denouement*, or conclusion to the plot of the main story and the frame story as well.

Wharton provides the final touch of irony when she reveals that the "querulous drone" heard by The Narrator comes from Mattie and not Zeena. Mattie has lost her sweet temperament and can be mistaken for Zeena. Zeena never changed from her sickliness, but she has put aside her imagined illnesses and her overdeveloped sense of self-pity to care for the two invalids.

Ethan, the most introspective and sensitive of the characters, has suffered a life in death after the smash-up. The repeated graveyard image is ironic because Ethan had twice speculated about his life in connection with the Frome graveyard. The first time he imagined himself living out his years with Mattie, the second time of enduring his life with Zeena. He did not suspect his fate was to be a nightmarish combination of the two daydreams.

The prologue emphasizes the themes of silence, isolation, and entrapment that Ethan has accepted as his fate because he was unable to violate the rules of society. Ethan did not choose to stand up to Zeena, divorce her, or run away with Mattie. He stood by his marriage vows, right or wrong, and as a result, will live out his life in silence and isolation.

Glossary

slatternly   having the habits of a slattern; dirty; slovenly; untidy

to'rd   toward

avowal   open acknowledgment or declaration

ha'   have

CHARACTER ANALYSES

Ethan Frome

Ethan Frome is the protagonist of the novel. A "ruin of a man," according to The Narrator, he is still a "striking figure." He appears to be tall, though his "strong shoulders" are "bent out of shape." He has blue eyes and brown hair with a streak of light. He has a "powerful look," that is "bleak and unapproachable." Everyone who knows Ethan respects his taciturnity. Ethan is a poor man who is simple, straightforward, and responsible. When The Narrator first glimpses Ethan's face in an unguarded moment, he sees Ethan as a man who ". . . looks as if he (is) dead and in hell. . . ."

Ethan's life has been quite miserable for over twenty years. As a young man, Ethan began college, hoping to become an engineer. His studies are interrupted by the death of his father. He succumbs to his sense of duty and cares for his mother, who is ill, and the family farm and sawmill. Aware of the isolation and loneliness facing him after his mother's death, Ethan marries Zeena, a cousin who nursed his mother. Ethan would like nothing better than to move away; however, Zeena will not leave Starkfield. She becomes a hypochondriac and Ethan finds himself captive to the farm, sawmill, and Zeena. To avoid saying things to Zeena that he doesn't mean, Ethan does not respond to her incessant complaining; instead, he suffers in silence. His external conflict with Zeena becomes an internal conflict also.

In Mattie, Ethan discovers a kindred spirit. She seems to understand him. Ethan experiences an internal conflict when he realizes that he is in love with Mattie. He feels that it would be unfair to Mattie to reveal his feelings or to provoke her feelings for him. Again, Ethan suffers in silence. He watches Mattie dance with Eady and feels jealous but is unable to voice his feelings; he is, after all, married to Zeena. Because Ethan never talks to Mattie about his feelings for her, he is unsure of her feelings for him. He agonizes, wondering if Mattie could ever love him. When he is around Mattie, Ethan feels a sense of mastery. For example, he feels protective of Mattie; he feels authoritative, important, and needed.

The feelings Ethan has when he interacts with Mattie are in sharp contrast to the feelings he experiences during interactions with Zeena, who has a way of demeaning Ethan with her control of him. The night that Zeena is in Bettsbridge and Ethan is alone with Mattie, he fantasizes that he is married to Mattie. When the pickle dish breaks, Ethan becomes assertive; he takes over and makes decisions. He tells Mattie that he will glue the red dish together the next day before Zeena returns home. Ethan's intention is to deceive Zeena and protect Mattie. In so doing, he is proving his manhood and his love for Mattie. Although there is no physical contact between Ethan and Mattie, their nonverbal communication reveals the deep feelings they have for each other.

After Zeena tells Ethan that Mattie will have to leave their household because a hired girl is coming, Ethan's antipathy for Zeena is evident. He shows his anger and realizes that he has lost; Zeena has conniving dominance of his life. His impulsive plan to run off with Mattie becomes another unfulfilled dream. A partial cause of Ethan's tragedy is that he does not plan ahead. Instead, he escapes reality through self-delusion. Ethan deliberates between doing what's right and doing what he wants. In the end, he submits to his obligations.

Ethan sees suicide as the only escape from the loneliness and isolation that has become his life. When the attempt he and Mattie make fails to kill them, Ethan reverts to his old habits: He lives out his days as a prisoner of circumstance, suffering in silence.

Zenobia (Zeena) Frome

Zeena's character is revealed through Ethan's memory and the action of the main story, and through hints from characters in the frame story. Wharton describes Zeena's physical appearance as gaunt, wrinkled, and sallow-faced. She has false teeth and her hair is kept in place with crimping pins. She is asthmatic and "sickly." She speaks in a plaintive, whiny drawl.

Zeena is seven years older than Ethan. She married Ethan, at the age of 28 (seven years earlier), after the death of his mother. Ethan wanted to move away from Starkfield, but Zeena did not want to live in a city where she would have no identity. Her hypochondria and her few legitimate illnesses serve as excuses for her to indulge in patent remedies and expensive visits to doctors at a time when Ethan is struggling to pay off the heavy mortgage on the farm and still maintain financial solvency. Because so much money was being spent by Zeena, there was no way Ethan could get ahead and realistically consider moving. Over the years Zeena becomes adept at using her illnesses to control everyone and everything in her environment. Her illness is the reason why Mattie must go and a hired housekeeper must come to take her place.

Zeena's rule over Ethan is powerful. She is seen as a "mysterious alien presence" and an "evil energy." Zeena is silent, secretive, and observant. When she does speak, it is to voice either a want or a criticism; consequently, before the arrival of Mattie, silence has prevailed in the Frome household. There never was and never would be any real communication between Ethan and Zeena. Zeena is intuitive; she notices everything and does not easily forget things. Ethan fears that she knows his innermost thoughts. The extent of Zeena's authority is such that Ethan and Mattie are both uneasy when reminded of her; Mattie can not even sit comfortably in Zeena's rocking chair while Zeena is in Bettsbridge. Ethan's last impression before the sled hits the elm tree is that he sees a horribly disfigured specter of Zeena's face.

Despite her undesirable qualities, Zeena responds to the tragedy with stoic endurance as she takes the responsibility for the care of Ethan and Mattie. Her thoughts about the smash-up are not revealed. Zeena continues to find fault and complain; however she is finally drawn out of her hypochondriac self-indulgence by the need to care for others.

Mattie Silver

Mattie is Zeena Frome's cousin. Her father had been the envy of relatives; he'd moved to Connecticut, married, and led everyone to believe his business ventures were successful. After his death, the family found out that he had mismanaged the money they had invested in his business ventures. As a result, their money was gone. The shame of this revelation contributed to the death of Mattie's mother soon after the death of her father.

At age 20, Mattie was left alone with only fifty dollars from the sale of her piano. She worked at odd jobs, and it was not long before she became ill. Mattie's relatives punished her for her father's mismanagement of their money by refusing to give her financial assistance. Zeena, however viewed Mattie's impoverishment as an opportunity and invited Mattie to move to Starkfield. Mattie became Zeena's indentured servant, working as Zeena's aide in exchange for a roof over her head and food to eat.

During the year that Mattie lives with the Fromes it is apparent that Mattie is "quick to learn, but forgetful and dreamy." She rarely completes her daily tasks; however, rather than listen to Zeena complain (and because he is in love with Mattie), Ethan steps in and "supplement(s) her unskilled efforts."

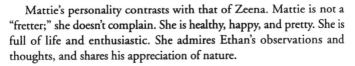

Mattie's personality contrasts with that of Zeena. Mattie is not a "fretter;" she doesn't complain. She is healthy, happy, and pretty. She is full of life and enthusiastic. She admires Ethan's observations and thoughts, and shares his appreciation of nature.

Throughout the novel, Wharton foreshadows the tragedy that befalls Mattie. Mattie feels insecure about her position at the Fromes because she senses Zeena's dislike of her. Several times she asks Ethan if Zeena's intention is to send her away. Mattie experiences an internal conflict when Zeena finally *does* want Mattie out of the house. Mattie doesn't know what she will do. She isn't trained: She has no money, and no connections to help her find employment. When Ethan takes Mattie to the train station (which they never reach), she declares her love for him and admits that she doesn't think she can live without Ethan. Their aborted suicide attempt transforms Mattie forever.

As a result of the accident, Mattie is paralyzed from the neck down. At the time of the Epilogue, she has lived with the Fromes and been cared for by Zeena for over twenty years. Mattie has become querulous, whining, and petulant. The beautiful, sensitive, and loving girl that Ethan fell in love with, in a sense, *did* die the night of the smash-up.

CRITICAL ESSAYS

Wharton's Style

Edith Wharton's writing style is characterized by simplicity and control. Her choice of vocabulary and sentence structure, which is as stark as the lives led by her protagonists, is deceptive. Throughout the novel, Wharton builds up patterns of imagery, patterns of behavior, and specially charged words; all of which serve a definite stylistic and structural purpose.

One of the best examples of Wharton's careful control is seen in the descriptions of the events immediately before and after the "smash-up." As Mattie and Ethan ride the sled down the hill, Wharton captures the initial thrill of the speed and then Ethan's frenzied determination to drive them straight into the elm tree. Her prose slows down as she evokes Ethan's return to consciousness. Not only in this example, but everywhere in the novel, her style is restrained, so that the way the words are arranged enhances their meaning without calling attention to the cleverness of the arrangement.

Because Wharton refrains from using unnecessary, superfluous modifiers, her descriptions seem to be almost elliptical or incomplete. She chooses adjectives and adverbs carefully and uses them infrequently. Her imagery is always appropriate to the limitations of her characters and is simply and subtly stated. For example, when Mattie and Ethan spend the evening together, Wharton uses the imagery of warmth and cold to complement characterization. She uses adjectives related to warmth when describing Mattie, and adjectives related to cold to describe Zeena. Other examples of elemental nature found in Wharton's imagery are stars, the seasons, animals, vegetation, light, and darkness.

Wharton's use of structure contributes to the depiction of Ethan's tragedy. The prologue and the epilogue, which take place some twenty years after the events of the main story, are written in first person from The Narrator's point of view. Structurally, these portions of the novel constitute a "frame" around the story itself; however, this frame is more than a decoration. The prologue not only establishes the nature of theme and action, but also begins the characterization of Zeena and Ethan Frome. It also sets the important patterns of imagery and symbolism and starts a tone of omniscient narration throughout the body of the novel. Ethan is the only character who is thoroughly explored.

Wharton's attention to minor details and her use of structure to relay Ethan's complicated and tragic life story to readers enables her to portray her characters as victims of the rules of society.

Literary Tools

Figurative Language

Wharton establishes patterns of imagery by using *figurative language*—language meant to be taken figuratively as well as literally. In *Ethan Frome*, Wharton's descriptive imagery is one of the most important features of her simple and efficient prose style. Her descriptions serve a definite stylistic and structural purpose. The figurative language used by Wharton includes metaphors and similes. *Metaphors* compare two unlike things without using words of comparison (such as *like* or *as*). For example, in the beginning of the novel, Wharton gives readers the feeling of the bitterness and hardness of the winter by setting the constellation, Orion, in a "sky of iron." When Ethan and Mattie enter the Frome household after walking home, the kitchen has "the deadly chill of a vault after the dry cold of the night." This image is appropriate to the living death that Ethan and Mattie experience in the years after their accident. Their lives do become cold and dead. The imagery associated with Zeena is bleak and cold also. When Ethan sees her before her trip to Bettsbridge, she sits in "the pale light reflected from the banks of snow," which makes "her face look more than usually drawn and bloodless." In contrast, the imagery associated with Mattie is associated with summer and natural life. Mattie's change in mood reminds Ethan of "the flit of a bird in the branches" and he feels that walking with her is similar to "floating on a summer stream." Later in the novel, when Ethan goes downstairs to tell Mattie that she will have to leave their house, their conversation has the effect of "a torch of warning" in a "black landscape."

Similes, comparisons of two unlike things that use words of comparison such as *like* or *as*, are direct comparisons that Wharton uses throughout the novel. At the beginning of the novel, Ethan's perception of Mattie's face is "like a window that has caught the sunset," and later, he thinks her face seems "like a wheat field under a summer breeze." As Ethan and Mattie walk home from the dance, Ethan reveals to Mattie that he had been hiding while she talked to Denis Eady. Wharton describes the moment when "her wonder and his laughter ran together like spring rills in a thaw." The dead cucumber vine at the Frome farmhouse looks "like the crape streamer tied to the door for a death." And, when Zeena tells Ethan that she should have sent Mattie away long ago because people were "talking," the effect of her comment on Ethan is "like a knife-cut across the sinews. . . ." As Mattie and Ethan approach their crippling accident, darkness prevails over the imagery. Darkness comes, "dropping down like a black veil from the heavy hemlock boughs." The black veil causes the reader to think of a funeral. Such figurative language evokes vivid images that reveal characterization and reinforce Wharton's themes.

Symbolism

Symbols in *Ethan Frome* enrich the themes found in the novel as well as Wharton's characterizations. A symbol functions literally as a concrete object and figuratively as a representation of an idea. Symbols allow writers to compress complicated ideas or views into an image or word.

The most important use of symbolic imagery in *Ethan Frome* is the winter setting, which is first described in the prologue and is carried throughout the main story. Harmon Gow's assessment of Ethan Frome early in the prologue is that he has endured too many Starkfield winters. From that point on, winter presides over the tragedy in all its manifestations of snow, ice, wind, cold, darkness, and death. The Narrator speculates that the winters in Ethan's past must have brought about a suppression of life and spirit. Winter is also symbolic of the isolation, loneliness, and immobility that Ethan experiences.

The name of the town, Starkfield, symbolizes the devastating and isolating effects of the harsh winters on the land and the men who work the land. The name is also symbolic of the stark and carefully composed prose Wharton used to write the story.

Other symbols include the dead vine on the front porch of Fromes' farmhouse that symbolizes the dead and dying spirits that inhabit the house and its adjacent graveyard, the farmhouse itself that has lost the "L" seems to be symbolic of Ethan (the house looks "forlorn" and "lonely"), it stands alone without support—isolated and lonely. The image of the butterfly, which has defied the cold and death of winter symbolizes freedom; freedom that Ethan is unable to attain because he is trapped in a loveless marriage. The cushion that Ethan throws across his study is the only cushion that Zeena ever made for him. Throwing it across the floor symbolizes his growing rejection of Zeena and his desire to run away with Mattie. Ethan thinks Mattie's hair is one of her most beautiful features; it is symbolic of her free, happy, and open personality. Zeena's hair, on the other hand, is always unattractively crimped and confined with pins, just as her personality seems pinched and constrained. The symbolic use of Mattie's hair is more important at the climax of the novel, when it represents beauty and love, to which Ethan is willing to give his love—but can't.

The symbols used by Wharton in *Ethan Frome* reinforce the themes of silence, isolation, and entrapment; feelings that Ethan experiences in his marriage.

Themes

Major themes in *Ethan Frome* include silence, isolation, illusion, and the consequences that are the result of living according to the rules of society. Wharton relies on personal experiences to relate her thematic messages. Throughout her life as a writer, Wharton would schedule the time that she wrote around social engagements and she did not readily discuss her writing. As a result, she was familiar with silence and isolation. The rules of society did not condone a woman who was a member of the upper class working, much less as a professional writer. Societal rules also frowned upon divorce. Wharton lived in a loveless marriage for years before she took a risk and divorced Teddy Wharton, her husband for almost thirty years.

Throughout the novel Wharton focuses on silence as a major theme. In the introduction, the author describes her characters as "granite outcroppings . . . half emerged from the soil, and scarcely more articulate." Each of the three major characters is encased in his/her own silence. Ethan, a quiet man by nature, returns to Starkfield following the death of his father to run the family farm and sawmill. Because he is too busy working to make small talk with the villagers and his sick mother stops speaking, Ethan becomes imprisoned in a "mortal silence." He experiences a brief reprieve when Zeena arrives to care for his mother; but after his mother's death and his subsequent marriage to Zeena, Zeena falls silent also. Communication between the couple is minimal and superficial. After Mattie's arrival, Zeena forces a smothering silence on her also with her "fault-finding (that is) of the silent kind." Ethan is able to share his passion for the wonders of nature with Mattie; however, when conversation takes a turn towards intimacy, silence returns and all Ethan can say is, "Come along." The characters are unable to communicate with each other to dispel their own loneliness. It isn't until Zeena forces Mattie to leave the Frome household that Ethan and Mattie express their feelings for each other. They abandon rational thought as they attempt to commit suicide and enter a silent hell in which the only verbal communication to be heard is Zeena and Mattie's complaining.

Isolation, another major theme in the novel, is not self-imposed before the tragedy that befalls Mattie and Ethan, but is enforced upon them by outside circumstances. Ethan tried to escape the isolation of Starkfield and his father's farm by going off to the technological college at Worcester. He began to cultivate his own social traits and to overcome his reticence; however, his father's death forced him to give up college and return to the farm and his ill mother. After his marriage to Zeena, Ethan is imprisoned by the farm, millwork, and caring for Zeena. He is physically isolated from the world at large and is also cut off from the possibility of any human fellowship that life in a village might afford.

Mattie and Zeena are isolated characters also. Mattie is isolated by the deaths of both parents and the ill will of most of her relatives. She moves to the Fromes', an unfamiliar farmhouse and, except for church socials, is cut off from contact with human beings other than the Fromes. Because Zeena is consumed by her many illnesses, she rarely leaves the farmhouse, and only speaks to Ethan and Mattie when voicing her complaints or demands. Because the attempted escape from isolation by Ethan and Mattie fails tragically, Ethan, Mattie, and Zeena are left to spend their lives in an isolation even more complete than that from which they tried to flee.

Illusion, a false interpretation or perception, is an important theme in the novel. Illusion affords each of the three main characters a means of escape from the reality of the silent and isolated lives they lead. Ethan would ". . . imagine that peace reigned in his house" when Zeena stopped watching Mattie so closely after her arrival. He wants to believe that Mattie's smiles and certain gestures are just for him. Ethan dreams of being with Mattie always; in fact, "he was never so happy with her (Mattie) as when he abandoned himself to these dreams." The night that Zeena went to Bettsbridge, Ethan imagines them (Mattie and himself) sitting "on each side of the stove, like a married couple." When

Zeena insists that Mattie leave their household, Ethan tries to convince himself that Zeena will change her mind. His illusion about running away with Mattie fizzles when he faces reality—he can not afford one ticket, much less two.

Mattie dreams of spending her life with Ethan. Ironically, her illusion becomes a reality. She does spend her life with Ethan, but as an invalid cared for by Zeena, not as Ethan's wife, as she had imagined.

Zeena's illusions are unhealthy. Her hypochondria enables her to escape into self-pity and self-indulgence. The smash-up forces her to abandon her illusions of withdrawing from all her household responsibilities through the device of a hired housekeeper.

The imprisonment experienced by an individual living according to the rules of society is a major theme in *Ethan Frome*. The message that Wharton conveys through Ethan is that when people fear they are violating the rules of society, they risk becoming enslaved by those rules. Ethan doesn't leave his wife because he feels bound by his marriage vows. He dreams about being married to Mattie; however, even as he writes his goodbye letter to Zeena, and subsequently talks to Mrs. Hale, his conscience does not allow him to follow through with his wishes. Instead, the rules of society rule his life and he remains entrapped in a loveless marriage.

CliffsNotes Review

Use this CliffsNotes Review to test your understanding of the original text, and reinforce what you've learned in this book. After you work through the fill-in-the-blank, identify the quote, and essay sections, and the fun and useful practice projects, you're well on your way to understanding a comprehensive and meaningful interpretation of Wharton's *Ethan Frome*.

Fill in the Blanks

1. During his stay in Starkfield, The Narrator lodged with _____.

2. The wealthy Irish grocer who has a crush on Mattie is _____.

3. Zeena was driven to the train station by _____.

4. Zeena went to Bettsbridge to see _____.

5. The Narrator gleans information about Ethan Frome from _____.

6. Zeena first arrives at the Fromes' to care for _____.

7. Ethan's dream was to become _____.

8. Mattie was going to be a bridesmaid for _____.

9. After the "smash-up," Mattie and Ethan are cared for by _____.

10. When Ethan decides to run away with Mattie, he is going to get payment for a shipment of lumber from _____.

Answers: 1) Mrs. Ned Hale 2) Denis Eady 3) Jotham Powell 4) Dr. Buck 5) Harmon Gow and Mrs. Ned Hale 6) Ethan's mother 7) an engineer 8) Ruth Varnum 9) Zeena 10) Andrew Hale

Identify the Quote

1. "He's seen too many Starkfield winters."

2. "Perhaps if it hadn't been winter, things would have been different."

3. "I've got complications."

4. "She needn't know anything about it if you keep quiet."

5. ". . . I don't see there's much difference between the Fromes up at the farm and the Fromes down in the graveyard . . ."

Answers: 1) Harmon Gow speaking to The Narrator about Ethan Frome. 2) Mrs. Ned Hale speaking to The Narrator about the "smash-up." 3) Zeena speaking to Ethan after her trip to Bettsbridge to see Dr. Buck. 4) Ethan telling Mattie that Zeena needn't know about the broken red pickle dish. 5) Mrs. Ned Hale speaking to The Narrator about Ethan and Zeena.

Essay Questions

1. The frame narrative is introduced in the Prologue. Why did Wharton utilize this technique?

2. Repetitive patterns of imagery are an important part of *Ethan Frome*. Identify several repetitive patterns or sequences. How do these repetitive patterns help the reader interpret character and action?

3. Explain how the setting of *Ethan Frome* contributes to the telling of the story.

4. Compare Zeena and Mattie both physically and psychologically at the beginning of the story. Compare them again at the end of the story. What ironic twist does Wharton provide?

5. Why does Wharton attempt to reproduce the New England dialect of some of the characters? What is the effect on the reader of the difference between the standard English diction of the narration and the dialect of the characters?

Practice Projects

1. Imagine that you were a newspaper reporter for the local Starkfield newspaper at the time of the smash-up. Write a newspaper article describing the accident.

2. It has been said that *Ethan Frome* is based on an actual sledding accident that occurred in Lenox, Massachusetts in 1904. Locate the original actual article and compare the actual accident to that of Ethan and Mattie.

3. Create a Web site to introduce *Ethan Frome* to other readers. Design pages to intrigue and inform your audience, include links to resources about Edith Wharton and other works by the author, invite other readers to post their thoughts and responses to their reading of the novella.

4. Rewrite the body of the novel as though The Narrator is curious about Zeena rather than Ethan.

5. Choose a character in *Ethan Frome*. Create a collage using magazine pictures to depict the personality of that character.

CliffsNotes Resource Center

The learning doesn't need to stop here. CliffsNotes Resource Center shows you the best of the best—links to the best information in print and online about the author and/or related works. And don't think that this is all; you can find all kinds of pertinent information at www.cliffsnotes.com. Look for all the terrific resources at your favorite bookstore or local library and on the Internet. When you're online, make your first stop www.cliffsnotes.com where you'll find more incredibly useful information about Wharton's *Ethan Frome*.

Books

This CliffsNotes book provides a meaningful interpretation of *Ethan Frome* published by Wiley Publishing, Inc. If you are looking for information about the author and/or related works, check out these other publications:

Critical Works about *Ethan Frome* and Edith Wharton

Zeena, by Elizabeth Cook. A retelling of *Ethan Frome* from Zeena's point of view. New York: St. Martin's Press, 1996.

Edith Wharton: A Collection of Critical Essays, edited by Irving Howe. Two of the essays deal specifically with *Ethan Frome*; others just touch on the novel. New York: Prentice-Hall, 1962.

The Two Lives of Edith Wharton: The Woman and Her Work, by Grace Kellogg, is a popular presentation of Wharton's life and writing. New York: Appleton Century Crofts, 1965.

Edith Wharton: A Biography, by R.W.B. Lewis, is an accurate biography of Wharton. New York: Fromm International, 1985.

Edith Wharton: A Study of Her Fiction, by Blake Nevius, is one of the best critical studies of Wharton's work. It includes in-depth observations on *Ethan Frome*. Berkeley: University of California Press, 1953.

Internet

Check out these Web resources for more information about Edith Wharton or Ethan Frome:

Edith Wharton (1862-1937), http://gonzaga.edu/faculty/campbell/ howells/wharton.htm — Includes links to Wharton's Homepage, biography, correspondence, and reviews of Wharton's works.

Edith Wharton, http://www.geocities.com/EnchantedForest/ 6741/ — Wharton's life overview, a list of her works, pictures, critical sources, links.

Next time you're on the Internet, don't forget to drop by www.cliffsnotes. com. We created an online Resource Center that you can use today, tomorrow, and beyond.

Magazines and Journals

Anonymous. "Ethan Frome." *The Nation*, October, 1911: 396-97. Internet: http://etext.lib.virginia.edu. A review of *Ethan Frome*.

Jordan, Kimberly. "Edith Wharton: How Society Influenced Her Writing." May 20, 2000. Internet : http://www.cwrl.utexas.edu/~tovo/auto/ spring/writing/research/kimberly/jordan.html. May 20, 2000. An essay about Wharton's life and influences on her life. A bibliography is included.

Other Media

"Wharton, Edith Newbold," *Microsoft Encarta 98 Encycolpedia*. CD-ROM. Microsoft Corporation: 1993-1997. A short biography of Wharton.

Ethan Frome. Audio. Read by William Hope. Produced by Nicolas Soames. Abridged by Sonia Davenport. Music by Tchaikovsky. Time: 2:38:41. Two CDs: ISBN 962634037 1. Two tapes: ISBN 962634537 3.

Ethan Frome. Touchstone Video. Directed by John Madden. Starring Liam Neeson and Patricia Arquette. Released: May 21, 1996 (original movie release March 1, 1993). Ninety-nine minutes. $17.99.

Wharton's Selected Works

Verses, 1878

The Decoration of Houses, 1897 (with Ogden Codman, Jr.)

The Greater Inclination, 1899

The Touchstone, 1900

Crucial Instances, 1901

The Walley Decision, 1902

Sanctuary, 1903

Italian Villas and Their Gardens, 1904

The Descent of Man and Other Stories, 1904

Italian Backgrounds, 1905

The House of Mirth, 1905

Madame De Treymes, 1907

The Fruit of the Tree, 1907

The Hermit and the Wild Woman, 1908

A Motor-Flight Through France, 1908

Tales of Men and Ghosts, 1910

Ethan Frome, 1911

The Reef, 1912

The Custom of the County, 1913

Fighting France, from Dunkerque to Belfort, 1915

The Book of the Homeless, 1916

Xingu and Other Stories, 1916

Summer, 1917

The Marne, 1918

The Age of Innocence, 1920

The Glimpses of the Moon, 1922

A Son at the Front, 1923

Old New York, 1924

The Writing of Fiction, 1925

The Mother's Recompense, 1925

Here and Beyond, 1926

Twilight Sleep, 1927

The Children, 1928

Hudson River Bracketed, 1929

Certain People, 1930

The Gods Arrive, 1932

Human Nature, 1933

A Backward Glance, 1934

The World Over, 1936

Ghosts, 1937

The Buccaneers, 1938

Fast and Loose, 1977

Index

NOTES

NOTES

NOTES

NOTES

CliffsN🕑tes™

CliffsNotes

LITERATURE NOTES

Absalom, Absalom!
The Aeneid
Agamemnon
Alice in Wonderland
All the King's Men
All the Pretty Horses
All Quiet on the
   Western Front
All's Well &
   Merry Wives
American Poets of the
   20th Century
American Tragedy
Animal Farm
Anna Karenina
Anthem
Antony and Cleopatra
Aristotle's Ethics
As I Lay Dying
The Assistant
As You Like It
Atlas Shrugged
Autobiography of
   Ben Franklin
Autobiography of
   Malcolm X
The Awakening
Babbit
Bartleby & Benito
   Cereno
The Bean Trees
The Bear
The Bell Jar
Beloved
Beowulf
The Bible
Billy Budd & Typee
Black Boy
Black Like Me
Bleak House
Bless Me, Ultima
The Bluest Eye & Sula
Brave New World
Brothers Karamazov

The Call of the Wild &
   White Fang
Candide
The Canterbury Tales
Catch-22
Catcher in the Rye
The Chosen
The Color Purple
Comedy of Errors...
Connecticut Yankee
The Contender
The Count of
   Monte Cristo
Crime and Punishment
The Crucible
Cry, the Beloved
   Country
Cyrano de Bergerac
Daisy Miller &
   Turn...Screw
David Copperfield
Death of a Salesman
The Deerslayer
Diary of Anne Frank
Divine Comedy-I.
   Inferno
Divine Comedy-II.
   Purgatorio
Divine Comedy-III.
   Paradiso
Doctor Faustus
Dr. Jekyll and Mr. Hyde
Don Juan
Don Quixote
Dracula
Electra & Medea
Emerson's Essays
Emily Dickinson Poems
Emma
Ethan Frome
The Faerie Queene
Fahrenheit 451
Far from the Madding
   Crowd
A Farewell to Arms
Farewell to Manzanar
Fathers and Sons
Faulkner's Short Stories

Faust Pt. I & Pt. II
The Federalist
Flowers for Algernon
For Whom the Bell Tolls
The Fountainhead
Frankenstein
The French
   Lieutenant's Woman
The Giver
Glass Menagerie &
   Streetcar
Go Down, Moses
The Good Earth
The Grapes of Wrath
Great Expectations
The Great Gatsby
Greek Classics
Gulliver's Travels
Hamlet
The Handmaid's Tale
Hard Times
Heart of Darkness &
   Secret Sharer
Hemingway's
   Short Stories
Henry IV Part 1
Henry IV Part 2
Henry V
House Made of Dawn
The House of the
   Seven Gables
Huckleberry Finn
I Know Why the
   Caged Bird Sings
Ibsen's Plays I
Ibsen's Plays II
The Idiot
Idylls of the King
The Iliad
Incidents in the Life of
   a Slave Girl
Inherit the Wind
Invisible Man
Ivanhoe
Jane Eyre
Joseph Andrews
The Joy Luck Club
Jude the Obscure

Julius Caesar
The Jungle
Kafka's Short Stories
Keats & Shelley
The Killer Angels
King Lear
The Kitchen God's Wife
The Last of the
   Mohicans
Le Morte d'Arthur
Leaves of Grass
Les Miserables
A Lesson Before Dying
Light in August
The Light in the Forest
Lord Jim
Lord of the Flies
The Lord of the Rings
Lost Horizon
Lysistrata & Other
   Comedies
Macbeth
Madame Bovary
Main Street
The Mayor of
   Casterbridge
Measure for Measure
The Merchant
   of Venice
Middlemarch
A Midsummer Night's
   Dream
The Mill on the Floss
Moby-Dick
Moll Flanders
Mrs. Dalloway
Much Ado About
   Nothing
My Ántonia
Mythology
Narr. ...Frederick
   Douglass
Native Son
New Testament
Night
1984
Notes from the
   Underground

The Odyssey
Oedipus Trilogy
Of Human Bondage
Of Mice and Men
The Old Man and
  the Sea
Old Testament
Oliver Twist
The Once and
  Future King
One Day in the Life of
  Ivan Denisovich
One Flew Over
  Cuckoo's Nest
100 Years of Solitude
O'Neill's Plays
Othello
Our Town
The Outsiders
The Ox Bow Incident
Paradise Lost
A Passage to India
The Pearl
The Pickwick Papers
The Picture of
  Dorian Gray
Pilgrim's Progress
The Plague
Plato's Euthyphro...
Plato's The Republic
Poe's Short Stories
A Portrait of the
  Artist...
The Portrait of a Lady
The Power and
  the Glory
Pride and Prejudice
The Prince
The Prince and
  the Pauper
A Raisin in the Sun
The Red Badge of
  Courage
The Red Pony
The Return of the
  Native
Richard II
Richard III

The Rise of
  Silas Lapham
Robinson Crusoe
Roman Classics
Romeo and Juliet
The Scarlet Letter
A Separate Peace
Shakespeare's
  Comedies
Shakespeare's Histories
Shakespeare's
  Minor Plays
Shakespeare's Sonnets
Shakespeare's Tragedies
Shaw's Pygmalion &
  Arms...
Silas Marner
Sir Gawain...Green
  Knight
Sister Carrie
Slaughterhouse-Five
Snow Falling on Cedars
Song of Solomon
Sons and Lovers
The Sound and the Fury
Steppenwolf &
  Siddhartha
The Stranger
The Sun Also Rises
T.S. Eliot's Poems &
  Plays
A Tale of Two Cities
The Taming of the
  Shrew
Tartuffe, Misanthrope...
The Tempest
Tender Is the Night
Tess of the D'Urbervilles
Their Eyes Were
  Watching God
Things Fall Apart
The Three Musketeers
To Kill a Mockingbird
Tom Jones
Tom Sawyer
Treasure Island &
  Kidnapped
The Trial

Tristram Shandy
Troilus and Cressida
Twelfth Night
Ulysses
Uncle Tom's Cabin
The Unvanquished
Utopia
Vanity Fair
Vonnegut's Works
Waiting for Godot
Walden
Walden Two
War and Peace
Who's Afraid of
  Virginia...
Winesburg, Ohio
The Winter's Tale
The Woman Warrior
Worldly Philosophers
Wuthering Heights
A Yellow Raft in
  Blue Water

Check Out the All-New CliffsNotes Guides

TECHNOLOGY TOPICS
Balancing Your Check-
  book with Quicken
Buying and Selling
  on eBay
Buying Your First PC
Creating a Winning
  PowerPoint 2000
  Presentation
Creating Web Pages
  with HTML
Creating Your First
  Web Page
Exploring the World
  with Yahoo!
Getting on the Internet
Going Online with AOL
Making Windows 98
  Work for You

Setting Up a
  Windows 98
  Home Network
Shopping Online Safely
Upgrading and
  Repairing Your PC
Using Your First iMac
Using Your First PC
Writing Your First
  Computer Program

PERSONAL FINANCE TOPICS
Budgeting & Saving
  Your Money
Getting a Loan
Getting Out of Debt
Investing for the
  First Time
Investing in
  401(k) Plans
Investing in IRAs
Investing in
  Mutual Funds
Investing in the
  Stock Market
Managing Your Money
Planning Your
  Retirement
Understanding
  Health Insurance
Understanding
  Life Insurance

CAREER TOPICS
Delivering a Winning
  Job Interview
Finding a Job
  on the Web
Getting a Job
Writing a Great Resume

CPSIA information can be obtained at www.ICGtesting.com
Printed in the USA
LVOW12s1201300913

354603LV00007B/159/P